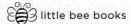 little bee books

An imprint of Bonnier Publishing USA
251 Park Avenue South, New York, NY 10010
Copyright © 2017 by Bonnier Publishing USA
All rights reserved, including the right of reproduction in whole or in part in any form.
LITTLE BEE BOOKS is a trademark of Bonnier Publishing USA, and associated colophon is a trademark of Bonnier Publishing USA.
Manufactured in the United States   LB 0517
First Edition 10 9 8 7 6 5 4 3 2 1

Library of Congress Cataloging-in-Publication Data:
Names: Ohlin, Nancy, author. | Simó, Roger, illustrator.
Title: The Space Race / by Nancy Ohlin; illustrated by Roger Simó.
Description: First edition. | New York, New York: Little Bee Books, [2017]
Series: Blast Back! | Includes bibliographical references. | Audience: Ages 7–10. |
Audience: grades 4–6. | Subjects: LCSH: Space race—History—Juvenile literature. |
Astronautics—United States—History—Juvenile literature. | Astronautics—Soviet Union—
History—Juvenile literature.
Classification: LCC TL793.O43 2017 | DDC 629.4/109046—dc23
LC record available at https://lccn.loc.gov/2017003458

Identifiers: LCCN 2017003458
ISBN 978-1-4998-0452-2 (pbk) | ISBN 978-1-4998-0453-9 (hc)

littlebeebooks.com
bonnierpublishingusa.com

THE SPACE RACE

by **Nancy Ohlin**   illustrated by **Roger Simó**

little bee books

CONTENTS

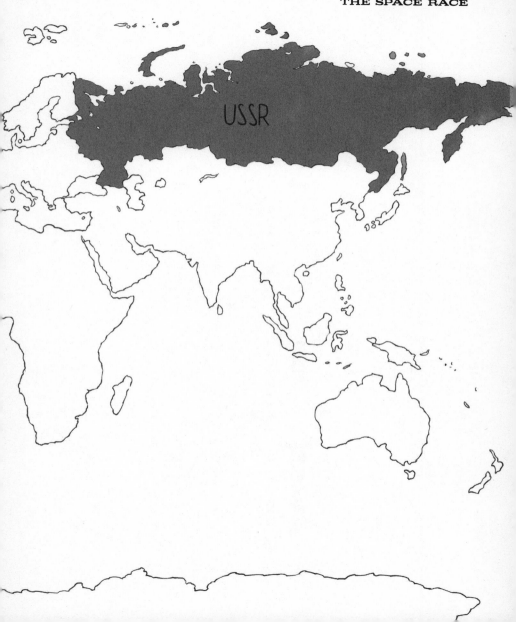

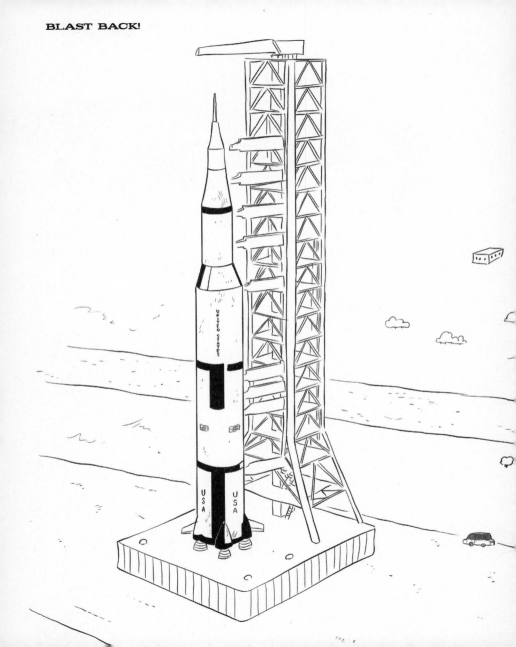

Introduction

Have you ever heard people mention the space race and wondered what they were talking about? Was it an actual race? Who was racing against whom? Who won, and what was at stake?

Let's blast back in time for a little adventure and find out. . . .

A Brief History of the Space Race

The space race wasn't a typical race. It wasn't like a car race or a running race.

Instead, it was a prolonged competition between the United States and a country called the Union of Soviet Socialist Republics (USSR) to see who could achieve superior spaceflight capability. It was part of a larger rivalry between the U.S. and the USSR that began after World War II.

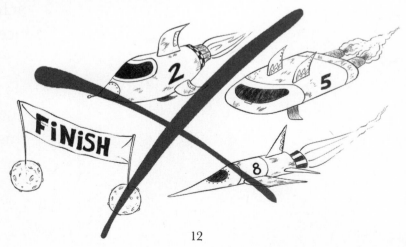

But the space race wasn't a typical competition, either. The U.S. and the USSR didn't publicly declare that they were going to compete to see which side would "win." Rather, both countries worked hard and often in secret to try to outdo each other—in space and also in other fields of science and technology.

The space race started in the 1950s and lasted for several decades. The U.S. and the USSR were the two biggest forces in space exploration during this time, although other countries eventually became involved, too.

Where Is the USSR?

The Union of Soviet Socialist Republics, also called the Soviet Union, no longer exists. The USSR, which lasted from 1922 to 1991, was made up of fifteen republics (or states): Armenia, Azerbaijan, Belarus, Estonia, Georgia, Kazakhstan, Kyrgyzstan, Latvia, Lithuania, Moldova, Russia, Tajikistan, Turkmenistan, Ukraine, and Uzbekistan. Today, they are fifteen separate countries.

Covering more than eight and a half million square miles, the USSR was geographically the largest country in history. It was also the first country to have a government based on the political and economic ideals of communism. (With communism, there is no private property; in the USSR, the Communist Party owned everything and ruled over everyone.)

Space Programs Around the World

Today, many other countries are involved in space exploration, including China, India, Japan, France, Germany, Italy, South Korea, Canada, the United Kingdom, Spain, Brazil, and Belgium. Still, as of 2013, the United States spent more on its space program than did all the other countries with space programs combined.

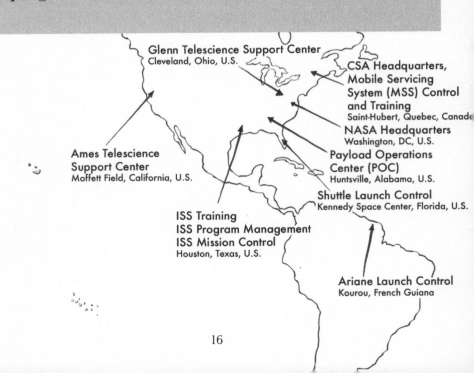

Glenn Telescience Support Center
Cleveland, Ohio, U.S.

CSA Headquarters,
Mobile Servicing
System (MSS) Control
and Training
Saint-Hubert, Quebec, Canada

NASA Headquarters
Washington, DC, U.S.

Ames Telescience
Support Center
Moffett Field, California, U.S.

Payload Operations
Center (POC)
Huntsville, Alabama, U.S.

Shuttle Launch Control
Kennedy Space Center, Florida, U.S.

ISS Training
ISS Program Management
ISS Mission Control
Houston, Texas, U.S.

Ariane Launch Control
Kourou, French Guiana

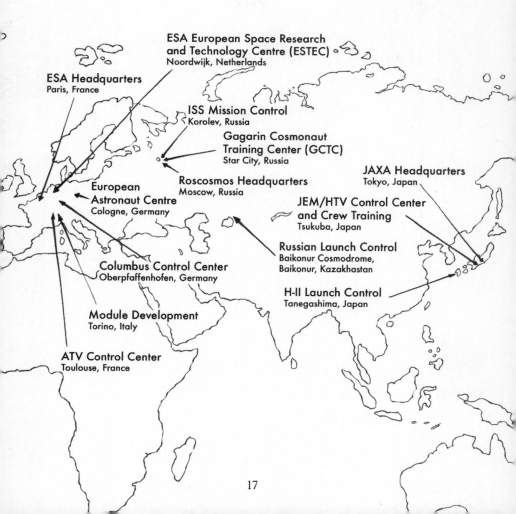

ESA European Space Research
and Technology Centre (ESTEC)
Noordwijk, Netherlands

ESA Headquarters
Paris, France

ISS Mission Control
Korolev, Russia

Gagarin Cosmonaut
Training Center (GCTC)
Star City, Russia

JAXA Headquarters
Tokyo, Japan

Roscosmos Headquarters
Moscow, Russia

European
Astronaut Centre
Cologne, Germany

JEM/HTV Control Center
and Crew Training
Tsukuba, Japan

Russian Launch Control
Baikonur Cosmodrome,
Baikonur, Kazakhastan

Columbus Control Center
Oberpfaffenhofen, Germany

H-II Launch Control
Tanegashima, Japan

Module Development
Torino, Italy

ATV Control Center
Toulouse, France

17

Why Explore Space?

Throughout history, space has been a source of great fascination. Ancient peoples looked up at the sky and wondered about the objects that appeared there. They marveled at the life-giving powers of the sun. They observed that the moon changed shape and position each evening. They noticed that the stars formed interesting shapes and they gave these constellations names and stories. They wrote about fiery orbs with tails that traveled across the sky.

The ancients were able to see the planets Mercury, Venus, Mars, Jupiter, and Saturn without a telescope. (The word "planet" derives from the word *planates*, which means "wanderer" in Greek.)

Until the sixteenth century, it was generally believed that the Earth was the center of the universe. In the 1500s, the Polish astronomer Nicolaus Copernicus refuted this, saying that the sun was the center and that every planet, including Earth, revolved around it.

The invention of the telescope (by Dutch eyeglass maker Hans Lippershey in 1608) took our understanding of space to the next level. Over the following centuries, scientists like Galileo Galilei, Sir Isaac Newton, Edwin Hubble, Albert Einstein, Carl Sagan, and Stephen Hawking discovered new planets and other celestial bodies. They also developed theories and technologies to expand our knowledge of space and lay the groundwork for space travel.

We continue to ask questions about space. What lies out there? Are there other life-forms? How can we travel farther into space? Will we ever be able to inhabit other planets? What can we learn about space that might benefit us here on Earth?

For the U.S. and USSR during the 1950s and 1960s, the exploration of space was a way to search for answers. But it was also a way to achieve world power and to try to avoid another world war.

What *Is* Space?

Generally speaking, space (aka "outer space") is everything that lies beyond Earth's atmosphere. The atmosphere is a layer of air surrounding Earth that gives us oxygen to breathe and protects us from the extreme heat of the sun during the day and the extreme cold during the night when the sun is on the other side of the planet.

The atmosphere is made up of five layers: the troposphere (0 to 8 miles above sea level), stratosphere (9 to 31 miles above sea level), mesosphere (32 to 53 miles above sea level), thermosphere (54 to 375 miles above sea level), and exosphere (376 to 6,700 miles above sea level).

There are different opinions about where the atmosphere exactly ends and where space begins. Some experts consider the Karman line, which is located around 62 miles above sea level, to be a good rough estimate. (The Karman line was named for engineer and physicist Theodore von Kármán, who theorized that conventional aircraft can't fly at or above this altitude.)

TROPOSPHERE

STRATOSPHERE

MESOSPHERE

THERMOSPHERE

EXOSPHERE

The Challenges of Space Travel

Why is space travel so difficult? Why is it impossible for humans and other living creatures to survive on their own beyond Earth's atmosphere?

Within the Earth's atmosphere and close to the planet's surface, we have oxygen and stable temperatures. We also have gravity, which is the force that ties us to the Earth's center and prevents us from floating away.

As we rise higher into the atmosphere, the air becomes thinner and thinner. Temperatures become more unstable and extreme. And as we eventually leave Earth's atmosphere, there is no gravity anymore to hold us down.

Spacecraft, too, rely on gravity to keep them in orbit around Earth. (Orbit means to go around and around.) Without gravity, a craft flying beyond the atmosphere and into space would simply drift away into the cosmos and disappear.

This means that space travel via spacecraft requires a number of conditions, including:

- The ship has to be able to defy gravity within the atmosphere (and fly upward), but then compensate for the lack of gravity once it reaches space.

- The ship has to withstand extremes of temperature and other hostile conditions.

- The ship (and also the spacesuits worn by those aboard it) has to provide an Earth-like environment inside (including oxygen, stable temperatures, and so forth).

BLAST BACK!

32

The History of Rockets

A rocket is required to carry anything (or anyone) away from Earth and into space. It has to be able to lift itself off and reach optimal speed quickly in order to defy gravity and reach space.

Here are some milestones in the history of rockets before the space race:

- In the ninth century, the Chinese invented gunpowder and later used it to fuel small rockets to be used in battle.

- In the late nineteenth and early twentieth centuries, Russian scientist Konstantin Tsiolkovsky developed a theory of rocket space flight that involved using liquid fuel that would be ignited in several stages.

- In March of 1926, American scientist Robert H. Goddard successfully launched a liquid-fueled rocket.

- In October of 1942, the liquid-fueled, long-range V-2 missile was launched for the first time. Developed by German scientist Wernher von Braun, the V-2 was a twelve-ton rocket that could carry a one-ton warhead. Later, it was used by the Germans against the British during the last years of World War II.

- In May of 1946, the WAC Corporal became the first American-designed rocket to reach the edge of space.

- In October of 1946, a V-2 rocket took the first photographs of Earth (from an altitude of 65 miles).

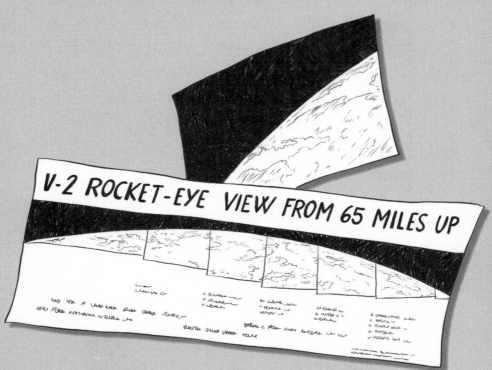

The Cold War

After World War II (1939–1945), the United States and the Soviet Union emerged as the biggest superpowers in the world. Even though they had been allies during the war, the two countries were very different. The USSR was based on communism. The U.S. had (and continues to have) a democratic form of government based on capitalism, which is the opposite of communism. (With capitalism, individuals can own property and businesses; with communism, individuals can't.)

After the war ended, both countries aspired to become *the* biggest superpower. This rivalry was known as the Cold War. The Cold War wasn't a war exactly, but a standoff between the U.S. and the USSR, along with their respective allies. Each side wanted to spread its ideals, influence, and form of government throughout the world. Each side also wanted to prevent the other from attacking them militarily, especially with nuclear weapons, which are far deadlier than conventional weapons.

The space race was a major part of the Cold War. Other aspects of the Cold War included:

- the arms race (to see which side could develop bigger and better weapons, especially nuclear weapons)

- espionage and counter-espionage (espionage is another word for spying, and counter-espionage means activities and equipment to prevent an enemy from spying on you)

- the building of the Berlin Wall in 1961, which divided the country of Germany into communist East Germany and noncommunist West Germany

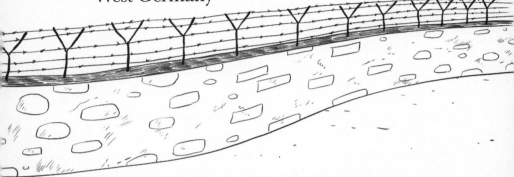

- the Cuban Missile Crisis of 1962, which almost drove the U.S. and USSR into a military war with each other

- the Vietnam War (1954–1975), in which the country of Vietnam was split into two: North Vietnam (which wanted a communist form of government) and South Vietnam (which didn't)

The space race was connected to the arms race in that the U.S. and the USSR both tried to develop space weapon technologies in the event that there was an *actual* war between the two sides. The space race was also connected to espionage and counter-espionage as both countries tried to develop ways to spy on each other from space. In these ways, the space race was very much about national strength and national security for both countries.

The term "cold war" was famously used by George Orwell in his essay called "You and the Atom Bomb." (An atom bomb is a type of nuclear bomb.) In the essay, Orwell described a "peace that is no peace" that would keep the two superpowers in a continuous and ever-escalating state of near-war.

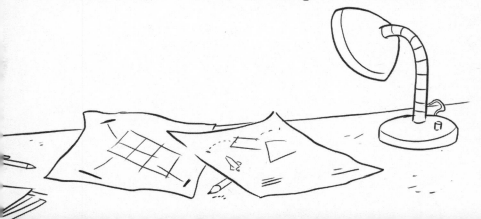

The Treaty on Open Skies

In 1955, U.S. President Dwight D. Eisenhower proposed an "open skies" plan to the USSR. The plan would allow the U.S. and the USSR to monitor each other's military activities using aerial surveillance (which means taking photos and videos from high up in the sky).

The USSR rejected the plan. However, the idea was revived several decades later, and in 1989, U.S. President George H. W. Bush signed an open skies agreement. In 1992, many countries around the world signed the new Treaty on Open Skies, including some of the former republics of the USSR.

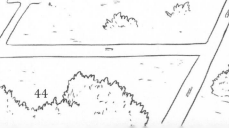

Sputnik

In the early years of the space race, both the U.S. and the USSR tried to be the first to develop a scientific or nonmilitary satellite. Neither side admitted that such a satellite *could* be used for spying.

The USSR won this leg of the space race when they successfully launched *Sputnik 1* into orbit around Earth on October 4, 1957. The USSR became the first country to send a human-made object into space. *Sputnik 1* was carried into space by a rocket that separated from the satellite up in the air.

Sputnik 1 was a 184-pound capsule made of aluminum alloy and other materials. During orbit, it reached an apogee of 584 miles. (An apogee is the farthest point from Earth while in orbit.) Its perigee was 143 miles. (A perigee is the nearest point from Earth while in orbit.) *Sputnik 1* made a full orbit around Earth every ninety-six minutes or so. It stayed in orbit until early 1958.

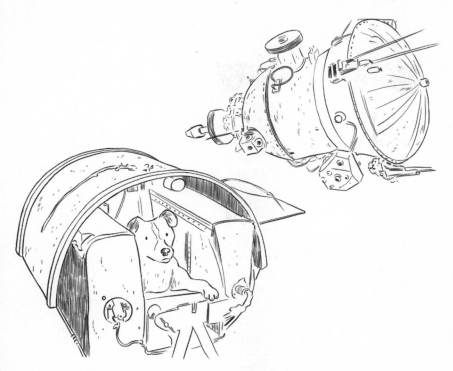

The successful launch of *Sputnik 1* came as a shock to the U.S. government and to its citizens, who had expected the U.S. to achieve this milestone first.

On November 3, 1957, just one month after *Sputnik 1*, the USSR sent *Sputnik 2* into orbit. A dog named Laika traveled inside *Sputnik 2* and became the first living creature to travel to space.

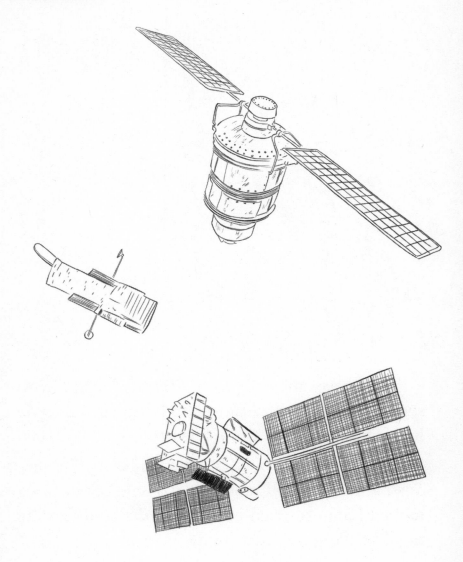

50

What Is a Satellite?

A satellite is any object that revolves around a larger astronomical object. There are natural satellites and artificial (or human-made) satellites. An example of a natural satellite is our moon, which revolves around Earth. An example of an artificial satellite would be a small spacecraft revolving around Earth.

Today, there are hundreds (if not thousands) of artificial satellites revolving around Earth. They are used for navigation, communication, monitoring the weather, military surveillance, and other purposes.

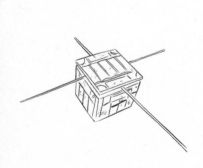

Animal Astronauts

Many animals have been sent both *toward* space and *into* space. The first animal astronauts were fruit flies that flew up in a V-2 rocket on February 20, 1947. (They reached an altitude of sixty-eight miles and came back safely.) Other animal astronauts have included dogs (like Laika), cats, rabbits, monkeys, chimpanzees, mice, rats, turtles, spiders, fish, and jellyfish.

Explorer

After the successful Sputnik missions, the U.S. scrambled to catch up with the USSR. Unfortunately, the unmanned Vanguard Test Vehicle Three (*TV3*), which was supposed to carry the first American satellite into space, exploded on December 6, 1957, just seconds after leaving its launchpad.

The Americans finally succeeded with an unmanned satellite called *Explorer 1*, which was carried by the Jupiter-C rocket. *Explorer 1* launched successfully on January 31, 1958, and achieved orbit around Earth. It made about twelve and a half orbits per day, collecting scientific information and sending the data back to Earth (including data about radiation belts that surround the planet). *Explorer 1* made its last transmission on May 23, 1958, but continued to orbit for twelve more years. It achieved over 58,000 orbits total before burning up on March 31, 1970, upon re-entering Earth's atmosphere.

After the launch of *Explorer 1*, there was an attempt to launch a similar satellite, *Explorer 2*, on March 5, 1958, but the fourth stage of its rocket did not ignite. The next Explorers were more successful: *Explorer 3*

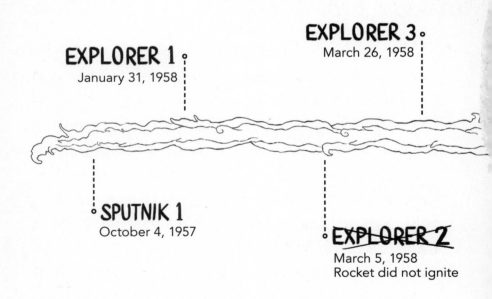

EXPLORER 3
March 26, 1958

EXPLORER 1
January 31, 1958

SPUTNIK 1
October 4, 1957

~~EXPLORER 2~~
March 5, 1958
Rocket did not ignite

was launched on March 26, 1958, and *Explorer 4* was launched on July 26, 1958. The attempted launch of *Explorer 5*, on August 24, 1958, failed during the separation of the second stage.

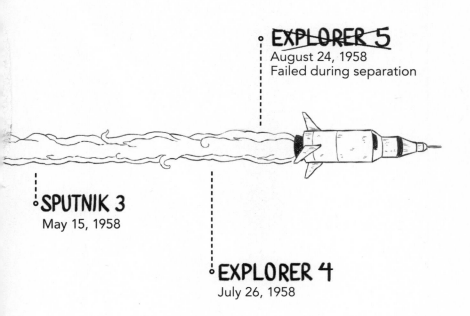

EXPLORER 5
August 24, 1958
Failed during separation

SPUTNIK 3
May 15, 1958

EXPLORER 4
July 26, 1958

Stages and Payloads

When a satellite is launched, the satellite itself is only a small part of the spacecraft. The satellite is attached to a rocket that ignites in several stages as it lifts into the air. As one stage of the rocket is discarded, the next stage ignites. This coordinated process ensures that the rocket's payload reaches its destination. (The payload is the cargo carried by a rocket—in this case, a satellite. Other examples of payloads include warheads, manned spacecraft, and fireworks.)

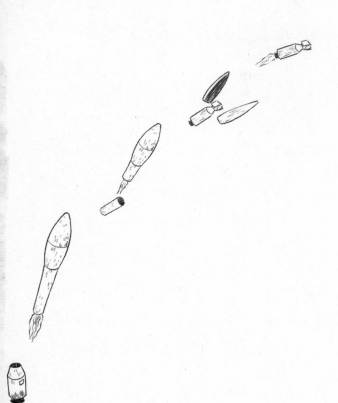

The International Geophysical Year

The International Geophysical Year (IGY) was a worldwide cooperative research program that took place between July of 1957 and December of 1958. Sixty-seven countries participated, including the U.S. and USSR. During the IGY, eleven areas were studied: auroras and airglow (a faint lighting up of Earth's upper atmosphere), cosmic rays, geomagnetism (the Earth's magnetic field), glaciology (the science of glaciers), gravity, ionospheric physics (the ionosphere is part of Earth's upper atmosphere), longitude and latitude, meteorology (the study of weather), oceanography, seismology (the science of earthquakes), and solar activity. American and Soviet artificial satellite programs (including Sputnik and Explorer) contributed important data to the program.

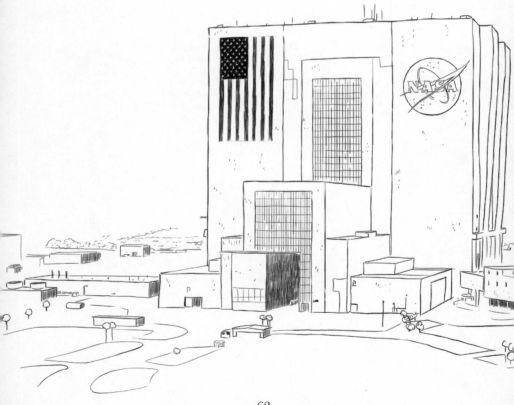

NASA

After the USSR successfully launched *Sputnik 1*, U.S. President Dwight D. Eisenhower was criticized for not making space a priority. In July of 1958, he announced the formation of a governmental agency called NASA (which stands for the National Aeronautics and Space Administration).

NASA still exists today. Its purpose is to research and develop the means to explore space. According to the NASA Web site, "We reach for new heights and reveal the unknown for the benefit of humankind."

A Race to the Moon

In 1959, both the U.S. and USSR set their sights on reaching the moon, which is no easy feat, as it's approximately 238,900 miles from Earth.

To achieve this goal, the USSR launched *Luna 1*, an unmanned satellite, in January of 1959. It didn't get to the moon, but it became the first spacecraft to go beyond Earth's orbit. It also became the first artificial satellite to achieve an orbit around the sun.

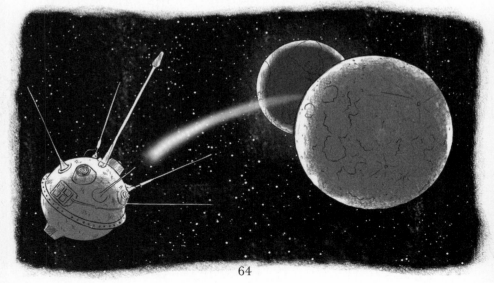

In March, the U.S. launched *Pioneer 4*, which was also unmanned. Like *Luna 1*, it missed the moon and fell into orbit around the sun.

That September, the USSR finally won this leg of the space race when its unmanned satellite *Luna 2* reached the surface of the moon. It was the first human-made object to land on the moon or on any celestial body in space, for that matter.

In October, the unmanned *Luna 3* was launched, and its cameras were able to photograph most of the moon's far side (which is the side of the moon that is always turned away from Earth). This was the first time the world had seen images of that part of the moon and was an important scientific milestone.

The USSR achieved yet another victory in the space race when one of its cosmonauts, Yuri Gagarin, became the first human to reach space on April 12, 1961. (A cosmonaut is a Soviet astronaut.) Gagarin flew the *Vostok 1*, a space capsule, into orbit around Earth. Now, the USSR was one step closer to getting a *manned* spacecraft to the moon. The Americans were determined to catch up.

In May of 1961, partly in response to Gagarin's achievement, U.S. President John F. Kennedy (who had succeeded President Eisenhower in January) declared a new goal for the country: that by the end of the decade, Americans would land a man on the moon and return him safely to Earth.

A little over a year later, the president spoke in front of a large crowd at Rice Stadium in Houston, Texas, in an effort to convince the Amerian public to support this new goal.

John Glenn

John Glenn (1921–2016) was the first American astronaut to orbit the Earth. In February 1962, he completed three orbits in the *Friendship 7* space capsule. (The first person in space, Soviet cosmonaut Yuri Gagarin, had only completed one orbit around Earth, in 1961.) Glenn became a national hero.

Glenn retired from the space program in 1964. In 1974, he was elected U.S. senator from Ohio; he was reelected for three terms after that. He also ran for president in 1984. In October of 1988, he became (at the age of 77) the oldest person to travel in space when he went on a nine-day mission aboard the space shuttle *Discovery* as a payload specialist. He was awarded the Presidential Medal of Freedom in 2012.

The First Women in Space

A brave Soviet cosmonaut named Valentina Tereshkova was the first woman to travel into space. On June 16, 1963, she went up in the spacecraft *Vostok 6* and achieved orbit around Earth. She went around Earth 48 times in 71 hours.

The second woman in space was another Soviet cosmonaut, Svetlana Savitskaya, who, in 1984, became the first woman to do a spacewalk. (A spacewalk involves exiting a craft and venturing out into space.)

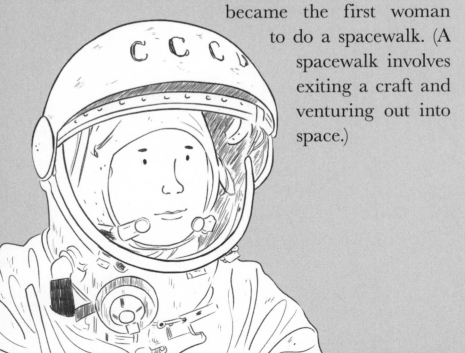

The first American woman in space was Sally Ride, who went up in the *Challenger* space shuttle in 1983. She went up again in 1984; on board was another astronaut, Kathryn Sullivan, who became the first American woman to walk in space.

Spying from Space

Between 1959 and 1972, the U.S. had a top-secret project code-named Corona, which was a series of secret military reconnaissance satellites. These satellites, also called spy satellites, are used to take photographs from space, communicate, eavesdrop, and collect important information (such as the presence of nuclear missile sites in enemy territory). The U.S. hid the first phases of Corona by pretending that it was part of a publicly known research project called Discoverer.

Between 1961 and 1994, the USSR had a similar top-secret project called Zenit. As with the Corona project, Zenit spy satellites were disguised as being part of a research project referred to as Kosmos.

Reconnaissance satellites still exist today. In the U.S., reconnaissance satellites are designed, built, and operated by a governmental agency called the National Reconnaissance Office (NRO).

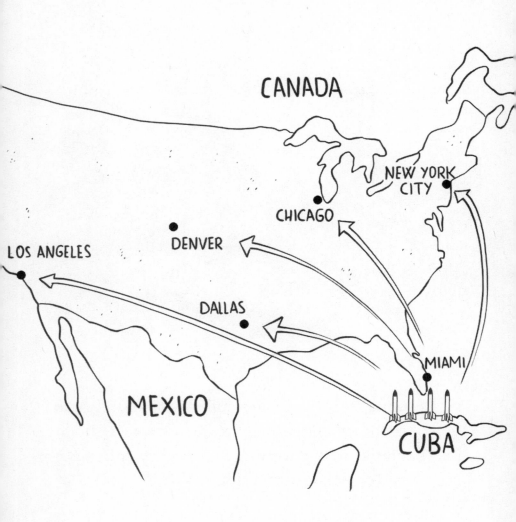

The Cuban Missile Crisis

In October of 1962, cameras on board an American reconnaissance aircraft photographed Soviet nuclear missile sites that were under construction in Cuba, which was a mere ninety miles off the coast of Florida. Missiles launched from these sites could strike much of the eastern United States within minutes.

This became an extremely high-pressure situation because if either the U.S. or USSR chose to fire a missile at the other first, the other country could retaliate, and thus start a nuclear war. (The U.S. had nuclear missile sites in Turkey near the USSR border.) To avert such a war, both countries removed their weapons from close proximity to each other and made other concessions as well.

The crisis lasted only for a couple of weeks. However, it was the closest the world had ever come to an all-out nuclear war.

The MOL Program

In December 1963, the American government announced plans to build a manned space station called the Manned Orbiting Laboratory (MOL). It would be designated for scientific research, but its secret purpose was to allow the astronauts to spy on the USSR and take better, more detailed photographs than the Corona satellites were able to.

The MOL space station was never built, however. The program was shut down in June of 1969 due to a reduced budget because of the Vietnam War, similar efforts already being utilized at NASA, and improvements in computer technology that eliminated the need for a *manned* spying space station.

BLAST BACK!

A Man on the Moon

On December 21, 1968, the U.S. successfully launched *Apollo 8*. It became the first manned spacecraft to orbit the moon and return safely. Then, in July of 1969, President Kennedy's legacy was fulfilled when American astronauts Neil Armstrong, Edwin "Buzz" Aldrin, and Michael Collins reached the moon in *Apollo 11*. Their spacecraft consisted of three transports: a command module (the *Columbia*), a service module, and a lunar module (the *Eagle*). It was launched on July 16 by the Saturn V rocket.

Collins manned the command module and orbited the moon while Aldrin and Armstrong went down to the moon in the lunar module. Armstrong became the first human ever to step on the moon's surface. Aldrin became the second. Collins took photographs and acted as a communication hub.

The three astronauts brought back the first geologic samples from the moon, including basalt (rocks made from molten lava) and breccia (rocks made from bits of older rocks).

This epic event is remembered as "one small step for a man and one giant leap for mankind."

Earlier, the USSR had been working on their own manned spacecraft to go to the moon, the *N1*, but it failed to launch. After *Apollo 11*, the USSR largely abandoned their moon program. However, in October of 2015, the head of Roscosmos (Russia's version of NASA) announced a new plan to send a manned spacecraft to the moon and achieve a lunar landing in 2029.

Since Armstrong and Aldrin, only ten people have walked on the moon (all U.S. astronauts).

The *Apollo 11* flight is considered by some to be the end of the space race, although Cold War tensions continued between the two countries for many more years.

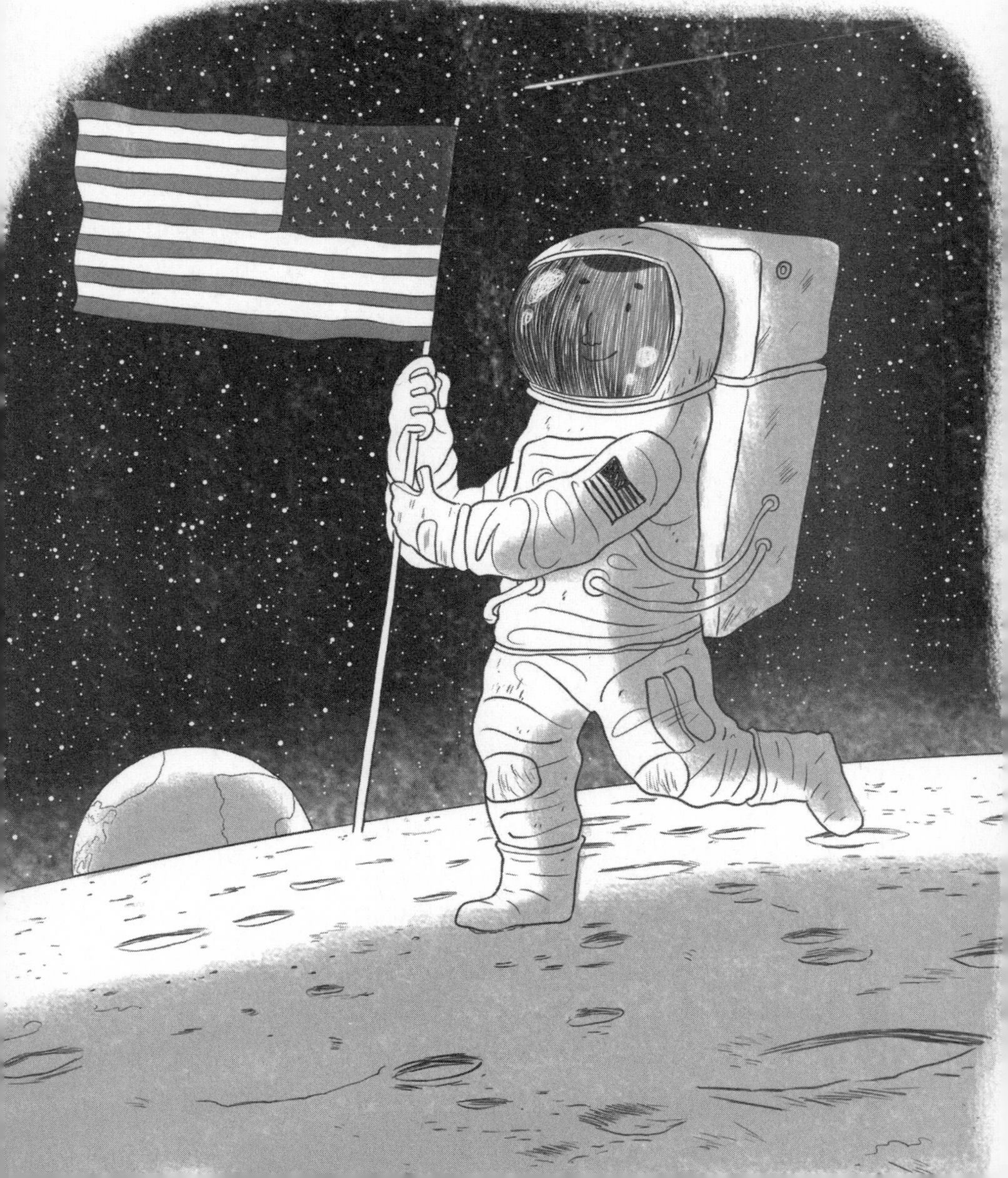

A U.S./USSR
Space Collaboration

In July of 1975, there was a first-ever joint space venture between the U.S. and USSR. The U.S. docked an Apollo spacecraft (an unnumbered command/service module) with a USSR spacecraft (the *Soyuz 19*) at an altitude of approximately 142 miles.

Up in the air, the hatches were opened, and the astronauts and cosmonauts visited each other's crafts, ate together, and exchanged gifts. They conducted experiments and learned from one another's work. At ground control (in Houston and Moscow), American and Soviet scientists tracked data together from the two spacecraft.

After undocking, the Apollo created an artificial solar eclipse by blocking the sun, which allowed the Soviet astronauts to photograph the sun's corona (an envelope of luminous gas that is normally visible only during a total solar eclipse).

The Apollo–Soyuz venture marked a brief period of goodwill during the Cold War tensions.

Between 1994 and 1998, there was another collaborative space venture, this time between the U.S. and the country of Russia (formerly a republic of the USSR). It was called the Shuttle–Mir Project.

The International Space Station

The International Space Station (ISS) is a space station that was constructed while in low Earth orbit, mostly by the U.S. and Russia, but with the help of other countries as well. It started out as an American project under President Ronald Reagan in 1984. Assembly of the ISS wouldn't begin until 1998, and it became fully operational in 2009. It contains a number of habitats, laboratories, and other facilities. Many astronauts have gone up to the ISS to conduct scientific experiments and perform other important work.

Ever since the U.S. Space Shuttle program was shut down in 2011 (after the space shuttle disasters of *Challenger* in 1986 and *Columbia* in 2003), the Russians' Soyuz spacecraft have been the only way for American and other astronauts to travel to and from the ISS.

The ISS continues to operate today. To date, the record for consecutive days spent in space by ISS astronauts is 340 days.

RUSSIA

ESTONIA

LATVIA

LITHUANIA

BELARUS

UKRAINE

MOLDOVA

GEORGIA

AZERBAIJAN

TURKMENISTAN

KAZAKHSTAN

UZBEKISTAN KYRGYZSTAN

TAJIKISTAN

The Legacy of the Space Race

The USSR ceased to exist in 1991 and broke up into fifteen different countries. Russia, also called the Russian Federation, is considered to be the successor of the Soviet Union.

The U.S. and Russia maintain trade and diplomatic relations, but the relationship between the two countries deteriorated after the rise of Russia's President Vladimir Putin (who has held office since 2012). They disagreed over many actions and policies, especiallly Russia's invasion of Ukraine.

Since the end of the space race, both the U.S. and the USSR (eventually Russia) have continued with their space programs. Many other countries currently have space programs, although only three (the U.S., Russia, and China) have achieved human spaceflight capability.

Since 1957, more than 6,000 spacecraft have been launched into space.

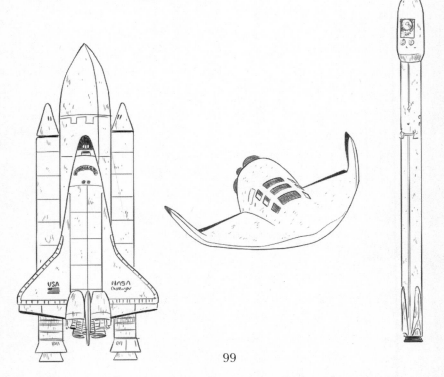

How Astronauts Train Today

Before going up into space, future astronauts must undergo many hours of training. The training can take up to two years.

Here are some aspects of modern-day astronaut training at NASA:

- Learning all about the International Space Station

- Flying the NASA *T-38* trainer jets

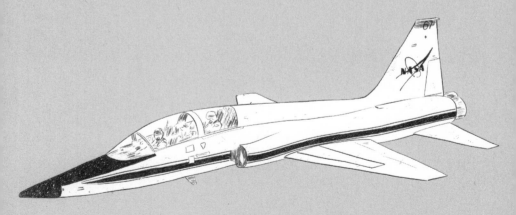

- Taking classes in subjects like science, medicine, and even public speaking. (If you want to be an astronaut on the International Space Station, you have to take language classes, too—for example, Russian, in order to communicate with the Russian cosmonauts.)

- Going through survival training.
- Practicing what it will be like to be in a real space vehicle by training in the Space Vehicle Mockup Facility
- Getting used to weightlessness in the KC-135 aircraft simulator, also called the Weightless Wonder or the "vomit comet" (because some people get sick in it!)

- Preparing for moving and working outside of a spacecraft by going underwater and performing tasks for hours at a time in a pool located at the Neutral Buoyancy Laboratory (NBL)

- Moving large, heavy objects on the Precision Air Bearing Floor, which simulates conditions in space. (It's like a really, really big air hockey table.)

Space Wars

Even though the Cold War is technically over, the U.S., Russia, and also China have been filling Earth's orbit with satellites that may or may not be weapons of war. It's hard to get an exact count because many of these spacecraft serve both peaceful *and* military functions.

The Future of Space Exploration

Great new achievements have been made in space exploration in the past few decades. We've reached and orbited Mercury, Mars, Venus, Jupiter, Saturn, Neptune, Uranus, and also Pluto. We've made contact with the surface of the first four planets, with one of Saturn's moons, and with an asteroid. We've taken photographs of the entire solar system. We've even grown lettuce in space!

So what's next? NASA is aiming to send humans to an asteroid and to Mars. There is an organization based in the Netherlands that wants to create human settlements on Mars. Other frontiers remain to be explored, including areas beyond our solar system. And scientists are always working hard to try to discover signs of life beyond Earth.

Well, it's been a great adventure. Good-bye, space race!

Where to next?

Also available:

ANCIENT EGYPT

by Nancy Ohlin
Illustrated by Adam Larkum

ANCIENT GREECE

by Nancy Ohlin
Illustrated by Adam Larkum

THE AMERICAN REVOLUTION

by Nancy Ohlin
Illustrated by Adam Larkum

THE CIVIL WAR

by Nancy Ohlin
Illustrated by Adam Larkum

THE TITANIC

by Nancy Ohlin
Illustrated by Adam Larkum

WORLD WAR II

by Nancy Ohlin
Illustrated by Roger Simó

VIKINGS

by Nancy Ohlin
Illustrated by Adam Larkum

THE GREAT WALL OF CHINA

by Nancy Ohlin
Illustrated by Adam Larkum

Selected Bibliography

Encyclopedia Britannica Kids online, kids.britannica.com

Encyclopedia Britannica online, www.britannica.com

ESA (European Space Agency) online, https://www.esa.int

"Here's where outer space actually begins" by Skye Gould and Sean Kane, *Business Insider* online, July 8, 2016, http://www.businessinsider.com/where-does-space-begin-2016-7

NASA online, www.nasa.gov

Smithsonian National Air and Space Museum online, https://airandspace.si.edu

"The U.S. still spends more on space than every other country—combined" by Roberto A. Ferdman, *The Washington Post* online, October 25, 2014, https://www.washingtonpost.com/news/wonk/wp/2014/10/25/the-u-s-still-spends-more-on-space-than-every-other-country-combined/

"Tracking Earth's Secret Spy Satellites" by Geoff Manaugh, *The Atlantic* magazine online, June 10, 2016, http://www.theatlantic.com/technology/archive/2016/06/mapping-clandestine-moons/485915/

"You and the Atom Bomb" by George Orwell, October 19, 1945, http://orwell.ru/library/articles/ABomb/english/e_abomb

"When it comes to war in space, U.S. has the edge" by David Axe, *Reuters* online, August 10, 2015, http://blogs.reuters.com/great-debate/2015/08/09/the-u-s-military-is-preparing-for-the-real-star-wars/

NANCY OHLIN is the author of the YA novels *Always*, *Forever* and *Beauty* as well as the early chapter book series Greetings from Somewhere under the pseudonym Harper Paris. She lives in Ithaca, New York, with her husband, their two kids, four cats, and assorted animals who happen to show up at their door. Visit her online at nancyohlin.com.

ROGER SIMÓ is an illustrator based in a town near Barcelona, where he lives with his wife, son, and daughter. He has become the person that he would have envied when he was a child: someone who makes a living by drawing and explaining fantastic stories.